Hamlin Garland:

THE FAR WEST

By Robert Gish

University of Northern Iowa

Editors: Wayne Chatterton
James H. Maguire
Dale K. Boyer

Business Manager:
James Hadden

Cover Design and Illustration
by Arny Skov, Copyright 1976

Boise State University, Boise, Idaho

Library of Congress Card No. 76-45134

International Standard Book No. 0-88430-023-4

Printed in the United States of America by
The Caxton Printers, Ltd.
Caldwell, Idaho

Hamlin Garland:

The Far West

Hamlin Garland:

The Far West

Hamlin Garland is regarded today with both condescension and respect. His Middle-Western writings, the early and later phases of his work, are more highly regarded than are the Far-Western writings of his middle phase. The cause of this unevenness in the Garland canon can be traced to his attraction to history and story, propaganda and art, Realism and Romanticism. The boundaries of fiction and non-fiction contract and expand throughout Garland's work, just as in his life he trailed and back-trailed from the Midwest to the East and West. In this sense Garland's writing is inseparably autobiographical and regional; and his search for the "right" literary form parallels his westering in search of identity and "home."

Although he was a "son of the middle border" and a "grandson of New England," he thought of himself and his art as Western, but he began his writing career in the East. From middle America, midway between the old West and the new, he looked, Janus-faced, at youth and middle age, backward and forward, with mixed hope and despair. As Donald Pizer, Jay Martin, and others have suggested, during Garland's early phase he attempted, in such books as *Main-Travelled Roads* (1891), to dispel the myth of the West as the land of success and the good life; yet in the Rocky-Mountain romances of the middle phase he nourished the myth. In his later phase he again demythologized the westering of his family and himself in *A Son of the Middle Border* (1917), *A Daughter of the Middle Border*

5

(1921), and *Back-Trailers from the Middle Border* (1928). Actually, Garland vacillates between praise and condemnation of the West and its "myth" even within his Far-Western writing. Moreover, Garland's interest in psychic phenomena, which dominated his old age, takes the themes of his later writings beyond the ambivalence he felt toward East and West, savage and civilized, fiction and non-fiction, into ghostly travelogues and ironies of the "unregional."

Because the scope of this pamphlet prevents a detailed consideration of all of Garland's writing—which in one way or another is "Western"—I intend to focus on Garland's middle period and his Far-Western writing in order to analyze his real and imagined "high-trailing." Also, because his trips to the Far West and the metaphor of the trail form the bases of his Far-Western writing, a consideration of his travel essays contributes to an understanding of his fiction. His real and imaginative journeys into the Far West take the form of an identity or vision quest and lead him nostalgically back to his youth and ultimately away from romance into the purer autobiography of *A Son of the Middle Border* and his own family's journey West. Whether fiction or non-fiction, Garland's writings deal with the constantly shifting location of the West as place and idea and with the need for each of us to find it for himself and to proclaim it dead or alive.

In "The Downfall of Abner Joyce" (1901), Garland's friend Henry Blake Fuller offers a satirical portrait of Garland as country boy turned "city slicker," at first scorning but then succumbing to the drawing rooms and feminine wiles of Eastern "decadence." That portrait has become the myth behind Hamlin Garland. Essentially a justified myth, it is promulgated by Garland and his critics.

Fuller's satirical portrait of his friend is not so critical as the negative reactions of many modern readers. Even some hostile dismay seems evident when critics like Warren French ask,

6

"What shall we do about Hamlin Garland?" Bernard Duffey is not alone in thinking that Garland betrayed his own belief in Realism in order to produce a long series of inanities. And William McCann agrees with Granville Hicks' indictment of Garland's career, which Hicks felt was one of growing sentimentalism and complacent garrulity (*Encyclopedia of American Biography,* p. 404). French goes so far as to say, "Even during Garland's most dynamically creative period, he was never more than a stylish journalist, obscuring his inability to get beneath the surface of experience by torrents of gush" ("What Shall We Do About Hamlin Garland?" *American Literary Realism,* 4 [Fall 1970], 287).

Those who view Garland as a shallow opportunist, less interested in literary principle than in turning a fast buck, point for evidence to his middle phase, which includes his Far-Western, high-trail, and Indian writings. His middle phase is bounded by *Rose of Dutcher's Coolly* (1895) and *A Son of the Middle Border* (1917) —both of which are often held in much higher regard than anything Garland wrote during the intervening twenty-two years. However, Garland's personal and literary escape to the Far West may be viewed not so much as a departure from what he was doing prior to and in *Rose,* but as a continuation; for he was building on the same themes of escape and of "making it," the same metaphors of journeying and climbing, that he was drawn to from his beginnings. Viewed this way, Garland's surprising about-face in mid-career from Realism to Neo-Romanticism is not so much a decline or fall as an excursion on the other side of what Charles Walcutt terms Naturalism's "divided stream." Regardless of one's judgment of their intrinsic worth, Garland's Far-Western writings are integral to an understanding of Garland, and more largely to an appreciation of Western regional literature and its relation to American literary Realism as they were developing at the turn of the century.

When considered in his historical context, Garland should be recognized as an important minor American writer. Charles Walcutt says that Garland's "inconsistencies" can be understood as resulting from "the impassable abyss that yawned between the genteel tradition and the first stirrings of naturalistic theory." Walcutt views him as an unsophisticated writer at the mercy of Victorian literary techniques, a writer whose works are "pathetic failures . . . painful first tries to break away from the genteel tradition" with only the idea and not the technique to make them live (*American Literary Naturalism, A Divided Stream,* pp. 62-63). And in writing about the late nineteenth-century Midwestern imagination, Larzer Ziff observes, "The function of literature was to take one away from oneself into realms of shimmering beauty and ennobling adventure. It was, on the whole, easier to go West to the Rockies and live that life than it was to go East and try to write of it" (*The American 1890's,* p. 78). Such a western turning—so well typified by Garland —was accompanied, Ziff adds, by a turning from Realism and Naturalism to Neo-Romanticism as a means of escape from the ravages of industrialism.

Garland's ambivalence toward Realism and Romanticism manifests itself stylistically, Ziff says, in the resistance of Garland's settings and characters to the creed he tried to impose on them. Consequently, he was forced to state a point instead of dramatizing it. He also had to use the vernacular along with grammatical constructions that reveal his own awe of genteel culture. Ziff reaches this conclusion: "After *Main-Travelled Roads,* regardless of what else happens in a Garland fiction, the language constantly betrays the realistic subject matter by coming to its aid with injections of loftiness. When finally, in the mid-nineties, Garland settled into writing romances about life in the Rockies, this was not so much a betrayal of his promise as an acceptance of the themes for which his language was better suited" (*American 1890's,* p. 99).

8

To Ziff's analysis should be added the observation that Garland's traditional narrative personae all address, explicitly or implicity, refined Eastern audiences—people unfamiliar with the glories and gaucheries of the Far West, people who need initiation into the more natural and primitive sublimities of the Far West. At the same time, Garland's personae suggest, they should not have to sacrifice their own culture and urbanity. Thus Garland's heroes and heroines are usually Easterners transplanted to the West or Westerners sojourning in the East. As a result, the plots of all his Far-West novels involve trips that lead East-West and West-East. They also involve journeys to new insights. The journeys even result in personality changes, where people gain whole new identities. Consequently, Doppelgängers and themes of duality abound.

Jay Martin sees Garland's double vision as reflecting "the characteristic tension of the regional writer—between his sense of a lost past and a present so debased that it shows no resemblance to that heroic past from which it has been severed" (*Harvests of Change*, p. 125). Numerous other critics, including Lars Ahnebrink, Jean Holloway, Edwin Neumann, and Charles T. Miller, agree that Garland's writings exhibit his ambivalence. They say that divided personal, critical, financial, and social motives all contributed to Garland's journeys to the Far West.

Garland's own life may be viewed as shaped by a series of journeys, geographically and psychologically trailing West in an escape from industrialism, but with intermittent "Abner Joyce" back-trailing to the East. Because of the close tie between his life and his writing, this nomadic process becomes a controlling formula for structuring his essays and, by extension, his melodramatic novels. Seen in this light, his Far-West period illustrates the fundamental ambivalences of his life and times. Garland divided his life along the lines of such journeys in his autobiographical Middle Border series, and an analysis of his

Far West writing shows him using the same sort of journeying in them.

In *Prairie Song and Western Story* (1928), a retrospective look at forty years of writing, Garland divides his work into four groups, each dealing with a particular subregion of the American Midwest and West through which he had travelled or in which he had lived. His grouping provides a helpful general view of his life and writings. First comes the coulee country around Onalaska, Wisconsin, where Garland's father, Richard H. Garland, settled in 1860, married Isabelle McClintock, built a cottage in Green's Coulee, and provided young Hannibal Hamlin Garland, his brother Frank, and his sister Harriet, with their first impressions of the land—impressions capitalized on in *Main Travelled Roads* (1891) and *Rose of Dutcher's Coolly* (1895). Second is the prairie, more specifically the area around Winnesheik and Mitchell counties in Iowa where the Garland family moved in 1869. They settled near Osage and stayed for eleven years, having the experiences celebrated in *Boy Life on the Prairie* (1899). The plains or short grass country of central Dakota, around Ordway, is the third subregion. Here Garland's father moved in 1881 and stayed for nearly twenty years. This area is represented as "the land of the straddlebug" in *The Moccasin Ranch* (1909), and is associated with the Wisconsin and Iowa experiences in *Main Travelled Roads*. The Far West during the late 1880's and the 1890's provides the locale for the last group of Garland's works, his high-trails and Indian writings.

Included among the other places of special importance in Garland's life is Boston, where he spent his apprentice years as a writer between 1884 and 1893. While there he attended the Boston School of Oratory and met William Dean Howells and other prominent authors. He established himself in Chicago in 1894 as a writer of the West. During his time in Chicago, Garland developed his friendship with Henry Blake Fuller and, in

1899, married Zulime Taft. He spent two of his early years as a writer in New York, and later, in 1916, he established there a home for his wife and two daughters, Constance and Mary Isabel. His last move was to California in 1929. Born in West Salem, Wisconsin, in the fall of 1860, Hamlin Garland died in Hollywood, California, in the spring of 1940.

Throughout his life, the Far Western works for which he is often scorned brought him some critical approval. In reviewing Garland's books of the Far West, William Dean Howells said that Garland was justified in being guided from West to farther West ("Mr. Garland's Books," *North American Review,* October 1912, p. 526). By 1916 Howells announced that Garland had attained his "rightful place in the sunset" beside Bret Harte and Mark Twain (William Dean Howells, "Preface," *They of the High Trails,* p. xv). He won among his contemporaries this "place in the sunset" as a Western author by carrying out a grand design for delineating the West, a design that began to take conscious shape during his many trips to the Far West in the 1890's. From childhood, however, the westering spirit had been in Garland's blood.

As related in *A Son of the Middle Border,* Garland's family theme song throughout his youth had been "O'er the Hills in Legion Boys!" in which appear the words: "Cheer up, brothers, as we go/ O'er the mountains, westward ho—." Moreover, Garland's graduation oration at Cedar Valley Seminary in Osage, Iowa, was entitled "Going West." As Garland viewed it, "Romance was . . . in the West" (*Son of the Middle Border,* p. 205). Based on the experiences of the "old soldier," his father, and on his own numerous moves as a youth, Garland saw in his western travelling his life's purpose as a writer: "to accompany my characters as they migrated into the happier more hopeful West. Like them I was 'Campin' through podner, just a campin' through' " (*A Daughter of the Middle Border,* p. 258).

Writing in 1892 about the West as potential subject matter,

and defining himself as one of the "literary pioneers of the West" for whom Whitman said he had been waiting (*Son of the Middle Border,* p. 256), Garland extols the West's magnificence: "For forty years an infinite drama has been going on in those wide spaces of the West—a drama that is as thrilling, as full of heart and hope and battle, as any that ever surrounded any man —a life that was unlike any ever seen on the earth, and which should have produced its characteristic literature, its native art chronicle" ("The West in Literature," *Arena,* 1892, p. 673).

Because Garland felt the need to delineate the West in fiction, he also saw that he must assess the achievement of his contemporary Western regionalists: "We have had the figures, the dates, the bare history, the dime-novel statement of pioneer life, but how few real novels! How few accurate studies of speech and life! There it lies, ready to be put into the novel . . . and it must be done by those born into it. Joaquin Miller has given us lines of splendid poetry touching this life, and Edward Eggleston, Joseph Kirkland, Opie Read, Octave Thanet, Miss Foote, E. W. Howe have dealt more or less faithfully with certain phases of it; but mainly the mighty West, with its swarming millions, remains undelineated in the novel . . ." ("The West in Literature," p. 673).

Garland's assessment of his fellow Western writers was based on his new literary theory, which he called "veritism." According to Robert E. Spiller's explanation of veritism, Garland "asked that American fiction divorce itself from tradition and imitation, that it explore truth to its underlying meaning, that it deal with the unpleasant as well as the pleasant aspects of life, and that it develop a form based on the moment of experience, acutely felt and immediately expressed" (*Literary History of the United States,* 3rd ed. rev., p. 1017). This "veritistic" theme surfaces throughout Garland's Far-Western writing as the would-be writers and artists in his novels serve as his fictive doubles. It is a propagandistic message he never tires of giving.

And fellow Western writers like Joaquin Miller and John Muir begin turning up as characters in Garland's novels as early as *Rose*.

Garland's plan to delineate in fiction "the mighty West, with its swarming millions" took shape when he began to depict such "types" as farmers, cattlemen, sheepmen, miners, outlaws, grub-stakers, remittance men, lonesome men, marshals, forest rangers, tourists, trail tramps, and Indians. In addition, his novels and stories show the role of women in an uncivilized, socially backward, masculine-dominated world. His fictional accounts of Western women were based for the most part on his observation of the lives that his own mother, sisters, and wife led "out West" where the spirit of place was supremely felt by both men and women.

In keeping with his theory of "veritism," as advanced most directly in *Crumbling Idols* (1894), Garland felt that a writer should try to record accurately the dialects of his region: "Nothing is of greater interest to me than the study of the direct dramatic, unconventional speech of the average man or woman. . . . The study of the West must, therefore, include not one dialect, but twenty" ("The West in Literature," p. 675). The essence of veritism, Garland believed, was to: "Write of those things of which you know most, and for which you care most. By so doing you will be true to yourself, true to your locality, and true to your time" (*Crumbling Idols*, p. 30). Understandably then, Garland travelled to the source of his fiction, to the actual Far West. He found the Indian, a figure he was increasingly able to feel empathy for, to be a crucial part of his design. By 1900, after his visit to the Standing Rock Reservation, the Indian aspect of Garland's Western literary enterprise became evident.

Taken chronologically by publication date, Garland's Far-Western fiction begins in 1898 with *The Spirit of Sweetwater* and ends in 1916 with *They of the High Trails*. Included within these dates are: *The Eagle's Heart* (1900); *Her Mountain*

Lover (1901); *The Captain of the Gray-Horse Troop* (1902); *Hesper* (1903); *The Light of the Star* (1904); *The Long Trail* (1907); *Money Magic* (1907); *The Moccasin Ranch* (1909); *Cavanagh, Forest Ranger* (1910); *Victor Olnee's Discipline* (1911); and *The Forester's Daughter* (1914). *The Book of The American Indian* (1923) collects stories written earlier. At one time, Garland felt that *Cavanagh, Forest Ranger* was the end of his Far-West phase, as he indicated in a comment to H. B. Fuller upon *Cavanagh's* completion: "I shall never do another book. I have finished what I started to do, I have pictured certain broad phases of the West as I know it, and I'm done. I am out of commission" (*A Daughter of the Middle Border*, p. 347).

According to Donald Pizer, Garland's depictions of the "broad phases of the West" combine three elements: "a mild conservationist theme, a sense of the glory of mountain scenery, and a conventional love plot" (Donald Pizer, "Introduction," *Rose of Dutcher's Coolly*, p. ix). The love plot follows a well-established tradition in the history of the novel. For in his "novels of the Rockies [Garland] used, as Walter Fuller Taylor has accurately noted, the conventional themes established by the Waverly romance—'flight and pursuit, courage and chivalric love, daring deeds of knights and other adventurers costumed as cowboys and ranchmen and soldiers and Indians'" (Jay Martin, *Harvests of Change*, p. 130). Edwin Neumann sees Garland's novels taking shape around stock triangular relationships involving hero, heroine, and villain, with Garland's hero functioning as the archetypal Western hero who was emerging in the fiction of the time (Edwin Julius Neumann, "Hamlin Garland and the Mountain West," pp. 63-64).

Garland felt that he had helped to establish the Western hero as an archetype. He says in reference to the genesis of Black Mose, hero of *The Eagle's Heart*: "I must claim priority over Zane Grey and other authors of 'Westerns,' as they are called in motion-picture circles. Owen Wister and I were early in the field. Emerson Hough, Harry Leon Wilson, and Stewart Edward White came later. Priority is cold comfort, but that is all I can claim in this contest" (*Companions on the Trail*, p. 14). As Jean Holloway notes, besides a common fascination with the West, Garland also shared with Wister an interest in the National Institute of Arts and Letters; and they were understandably good friends (*Hamlin Garland*, pp. 131, 156, 193). Garland's claim to priority may have been meant to suggest that Black Mose of *The Eagle's Heart* (1900) had a direct influence on Wister's conception of his "horseman of the plains," who appeared in *The Virginian* (1902). Although I cannot offer a detailed comparison of the two novels within the space of this study, I can say that there are recognizable similarities in terms of the characters, actions, and themes of the novels.

Garland based his fictional heroes on his observations of people he had encountered. Consequently, his Far West novels are best understood against the background of his travels there. His wanderings took him to the central and southwestern Rocky Mountain states, California, the Pacific Northwest, British Columbia, and more than a dozen Indian reservations.

A November-December 1892 family trip to visit his uncle, David Garland, in Santa Barbara, resulted in one of Garland's first Far-Western travel pieces, "Western Landscapes," published in the *Atlantic Monthly*. One of his most significant trips, in terms of the impact of the land on his sensibilities, it is matched in romantic impact by his "honeymoon" trip to Arizona, New Mexico, and Colorado in October and November of 1899.

In 1895, Garland went to the Southwest with two artists, Herman MacNeill and Charles Francis Browne, expressly to see the Moki snake dance, but with stops at Isleta, Laguna, Zuni, and Acoma pueblos. He must have gathered a great deal of source material, for this trip figures largely in many of Garland's Far-West stories, especially in his prototypic Western, *The Eagle's Heart*.

His 1896-97 trip to the Dakotas, Montana, and the Lame Deer Reservation also provided information for less notable fictional use. His extended 1898 trip to the Northwest and Canada resulted in *The Long Trail* and *The Trail of the Goldseekers* (1899). In the spring of 1900 he visited the Southern Cheyennes and Arapahoes in Darlington, Oklahoma, and there he listened to John H. Seeger's stories about the Indian way. During the summer of the same year he went to Standing Rock and talked with Slohan about Sitting Bull. These visits provided the material for his longest Indian story, "The Silent Eaters."

His travel essays foreshadow the fiction, for in the essays about these trips one can witness an accumulation of concerns and narrative devices drawing him inevitably across the border of autobiography and into the more spacious region of fiction. This passage into fiction is perhaps the most significant of his many journeys, because a quarter of a century later he would cross the line back into autobiography with a truer sense of himself as a son not of the Far-Western region but of the "Middle Border."

In most of what he wrote, Garland relied on the language of travel. A quick glance at the titles of all his writings shows the high frequency of words like "roads," "roadside," "trail," "trailers," and "travelled." The stock metaphor of life's "journey" sees extra duty in Garland's writing. He also frequently used such related ideas as flight, climbing, acceleration, deceleration, ascent, and descent. Travel from the plains and prairies of the Midwest to the mountains and deserts of the Far West is naturally complementary to such concerns.

Garland adapted a whole series of metaphors and images associated with the idea of traveling or "trailing." If one were to compile a Garland bestiary, the eagle and lion would take precedence, along with the horse. As for machines, the "iron horse" or locomotive is at once both antagonistic and companionable as a symbol and metaphor of progress and destruction. References to the various operations and movements of mining, with its vertical orientation, occupy considerable space in Garland's works.

In "Hitting the Trail," Garland pointedly defines what the trail as idea and experience means to him. What he expresses in this essay has an all-encompassing bearing on his Far-West travelogues and fiction. The trail for Garland is not restricted to any one place. It offers itself as a means of communication in a language of its own, functioning as it does as one large metaphor composed of a number of smaller ones. His intent in the essay is to explain that to "hit the trail" is an expression with numerous meanings, "a long train of related pictures, signs, and symbols" (*McClure's*, 12 [February 1899], 298). Elaborating upon the significance of these signs and symbols, he argues that regardless of how the trail is perceived, it is not lawless. Instead, it offers a fundamental temporal and spatial sequence of beginnings and endings, past and present, here and there. Furthermore, he argues that in America the trail is associated with connections between the animal and the human and the "red" Indian and the "white" man.

In terms of the road to progress, Garland sides with the Indian rather than with the white trail. The "red" trail, he says, is "always indirect, accommodating, patient of obstruction—an adjustment, not a ravage. It alarms nothing. It woos every wild thing. It never disfigures. It sacrifices itself. It loses itself in nature" (pp. 299-300). For Garland, "The Trail is poetry; a wagon road is prose; the railroad, arithmetic" (p. 300).

The trail, above all, brings change to the trailer. Garland thinks of changes in terms of character, conscience, and "overall manhood." Although the tendency of a man on the trail is "to revert to a state of primitive savagery," he maintains paradoxically that life on the trail also brings knowledge, pleasure, and peace of mind. In explaining the reasons for his own travels into the Far West and for his writings about the trail, he says, "It has given me blessed release from care and worry and the troubled thinking of our modern day. It has been a return to the primitive and the peaceful. Whenever the pressures of our complex city life thin my blood and benumb my brain, I seek relief on the trail; and when I hear the coyote waking to the yellow dawn my cares fall from me—I am happy" (p. 304). Here in essence is Garland's celebration of that part of his "myth" in which he sees himself as a traveller on the "sunset trail." But it is worth noting, too, that his "trail" connects with the city and that, though leaving suggests returning, "home" for Garland was really the process of travelling itself. A repeated cycle of leaving and returning became the ideal pattern for his life. The trail West thus functions for Garland as both structure and process.

"Into the Happy Hunting-Grounds of the Utes" was the first in a series of travel essays dealing with his 1895 trip to the Southwest. Garland dramatized himself as a heroic, "hardy horseman," on the trail over Colorado's White River plateau. In the face of his "Abner Joyce" self and the less robust readers of *Harper's Weekly*, he celebrates the mountains, his guide, Ed, and the joyful ambiance of life on the Far-West trail. In a nostalgic return to the days of *Boy Life on the Prairie,* Garland heralds his freedom: "I was a horse again! The reins fell naturally into my left hand; my knees took hold upon the saddle with joy. I thought of my prairie life, of glorious rides in the sierras, and I faced the peaks with delight, to be uttered only in shouts" (*Harper's Weekly,* April 11, 1896, p. 350).

Awestruck by the mystery of the wilderness, Garland describes fleeting images of scene and character, which he later put to fictional use. Feeling strongly the presence of trails past, he utters a plea in the face of a vanishing West: "Bring back the Utes who broken-heartedly fired their forests in face of the white men and retreated! Bring back the men to whom this land belongs! Silence the saw and engine; let there be one unapproachable wilderness left in America, one spot unmarred by greed and hatred!" (p. 350). This plea for the Native American way and for an ecological view of life finds expression throughout the later novels.

Amidst the trail talk around the campfire at night, Garland revels in his escape from civilization. With romantic fervor, he idealizes the men around the fire as being epic trailers and heroic Americans who are worth identifying with. Ed, the guide, is one such hero—like the Ute and the wilderness, he is a "survivor" destined for extinction. A "Hoosier" who had headed West and punched cows in Wyoming, Colorado, Utah, and New Mexico, Ed is the living prototype for Black Mose and other Far-West heroes of Garland's fiction. Moreover, one can see in Ed many of the qualities of Garland's own soldier father and of Garland himself.

Although a stranger to the wilderness and to Ed's life, Garland momentarily recaptures boyhood and the lost West by becoming both Indian and cowboy, transcending time and space by means of "hitting the trail." With his lyricism rising in high romantic swells, trance-like, Garland exclaims, "Oh the beauty and marvel of it! To be permitted to go back there into the past . . . was like a vision of death turning to be a dream merely" (p. 351). A similar nostalgia characterizes the trail that Garland followed in shaping these experiences into fiction.

Not published until 1899 in *Century Magazine,* Garland's "The Ute Lover" is nevertheless a poetic companion piece to "Into the Happy Hunting-Grounds of the Utes." But in the poem he treats the theme of love between man and woman, a prominent theme in his fiction. Garland was inspired to write "The Ute Lover" by that trip in 1895 when he and his artist friends moved south from Cripple Creek across Marshall Pass into Ouray and Silverton. They stopped at the Southern Colorado Ute Agency where they soaked themselves "in the sunshine and silence of the noons, and absorbed the moonlit, song-filled mystery of the nights" (*Roadside Meetings,* pp. 291-92).

Garland's song, reflecting the attitudes of so many of his novels, is a love lament for the passing of the Ute's mountain home, an expression of yearning for the primitively beautiful Far West. In presenting a Ute lover calling his mate, Garland becomes a "lover" of sorts himself, writing about his own ambivalent romance with both East and West and about the Far West's meaning to him.

In the poem, the music of the Ute lover is associated with shade and water, and it functions as a spiritual trail between his people's home in the mountains and their present desert exile. "The Ute Lover" is a prime example of Garland's fondness for linking romantic love and the spirit of place. For Garland, romance between man and woman is contingent upon the woman's accepting and, in effect, falling in love with the land.

In August 1895, Garland and his friends continued their travels down the Rio Grande to Isleta and experienced at first hand the life of the Indians there. Garland is not without fear —whether actually or for rhetorical effect—in his encounter with the people he finds. His account reflects his exaggerated and stylized Eastern narrative stance, and it emphasizes his ambivalence toward the region and its people: "suborning" a young Indian who spoke "comprehensible western American" as guide ("A Day at Isleta," *Southwestern Historical Quarterly,* 77 [July 1974], 48-49). Here Garland paternalistically joined the "red" and "white" trails.

Following a narrative structure, common to much travel writing, of describing a day's trip within a longer trip into a foreign land, Garland travels mystically back in time: "Low walls of gray mud shut out the world we knew—the world of the gringo. With incredible swiftness we retreated into the past. It was as if the boy [guide] were some mighty conjurer" (p. 49).

When he sees Isletan women threshing wheat, he retreats, in a sustained transcendent moment, so far as to the beginnings of agriculture. That night, he narrates, as though in a reverie, the story of Isleta, and how it suffered from the military encroachments of Spaniards and the Apache and Navajo tribes, and from the greed and lust of the Yankee. By way of benediction he says to the Indians: "There is sorrow before both man and maid, but my voice is for youth—my feet are set his way and my hand-clasp is for him" (p. 68). The implicit trail metaphor here is one that leads to his Indian fiction, as Garland sets his feet on the Indian's trail and thereby paradoxically argues the Indian's need to walk the white man's trail.

Garland wished to see the Moki snake dances at Walpi and felt that they would be the high point of his 1895 trip to the Far West. *Harper's Weekly* published his description of the visit in its August 15, 1896 issue. The metaphor of the trail and his feelings of empathy and transcendence again provided Garland with a narrative structure for his essay. Here more than anywhere else in the series of his travel essays published in 1895, he achieves a progressively dramatic effect involving mounting tension toward participation and arrival. Like so many travellers in American literature, he looks from the outside into a "savage," "new" world. Day by day he describes not only his penetration "into" the mysteries of the Far West, as with the Colorado Utes and pueblo Indians of New Mexico, but also his complete absorption "among" the Moki. By means of a transcendent moment experienced while watching the dance, Garland becomes part of the primitive, timeless life of the Moki.

Garland's account is evidence of his sincerity in attempting in his fiction to assume "veritistically" the personae of Indians. However sincere, his attempts were not always convincing. Drawn into the story of the settlement of Ha-no and the wanderings of its people as told by "Polaka," Garland fumbles with an Indian voice: "My people came from the East. Ho-pee say:

'You stay here; allee time keep trail; fight. Navajo no come, Ute no come. We give you land, we glad you here!' " ("Among the Moki Indians," p. 802). Despite his apparent inability to assume an Indian voice, Garland was captivated by the myths of travel and trailing. He learned the stories of Tiyo, the Antelope race, and the dance of Bearman, which lie in mythic time as the foundations of the Snake Dance.

In Garland's best Indian work, "The Silent Eaters," the travels involve the Sioux's Canadian sanctuary and the Western Messiah of the Ghost Dance. Similarly, the mythic journey recounted by the Moki was for Garland very significant. Though a twentieth-century tourist, he felt that he, too, was part of Tiyo's trip down the Grand Canyon to the ocean to see where the waters run. Garland's own adventures while "hitting the trail" are made to seem modern copies of such archetypes as Tiyo's marriage to two sisters who turned into two water snakes, the ones which the Snake Dance evokes, and his general adventure of exploration.

These travel writings of Garland not only provide interesting descriptions, but they also afford insights into Garland's fiction of the Far West. They help to explain the reasons for the "myth" of his own life as a traveller and "literary pioneer of the West."

The best place to begin in an analysis of Garland's Far-West novels is *The Eagle's Heart* (1900). Here Garland develops the conventions and forms that he uses in his subsequent Westerns and that, as he claims, anticipate (albeit in limited ways) the works of Zane Grey, Owen Wister, and others. The protagonist of *The Eagle's Heart* typifies the courageous, self-reliant, lonesome cowboy trailing into the mountains, escaping a confining guilt-ridden past for freedom under the Big Sky. In rendering Black Mose and countless other characters, Garland utilizes the eagle as symbolic spirit of the Far West. Garland says about the book: "It was an adventure story based upon the lives of my playmates in Osage, Iowa (most of whom hoped at some time to run away and become scouts or cowboys), and was my attempt at delineating the homely genesis of a 'bad man' " (*Companions on the Trail,* p. 13). Autobiographically, it is a projection of Garland's own feelings about trailing Far West, as evidenced in his travel writing.

Black Mose's numerous identities, aliases, and metamorphoses illustrate in typical Garland fashion the transforming powers of the primitive West and of a virtuous, "civilized" woman. Beginning as Harold Excell, then Harry Excell, Moses N. Hardluck, Mose Harding, Black Mose, Hank Jones, and then Harold Excell once more, Garland's good-bad hero hits three basic West-East-West trails, those of escape and notoriety, failure and illness, and then marriage and success. With some variation, such a pattern is fundamental to all Garland's novels about the Far West.

As his name suggests, Harold Excell, protagonist and man of many names, is "on the make." Though his ambitions lead him to seek adventure in the Far West, he finds true happiness only with Mary Yardwell and, as her name suggests, domesticity. They find a happy domesticity not in their Midwest home, but in the Far West, where Harold becomes a beneficent Indian agent. Of the many pursuits in the book, the main one involves Harold's pursuit of Mary. First he woos as a preacher's son gone wrong, then as a drifter and cowboy "outlaw," and finally as a white chief of Talfeather's people.

Linked with the trail metaphor is the process associated with "Excell" as an "eagle" soaring from the Midwest upward to the Rockies, then falling momentarily down to the plains, but soaring again to the heights of the American dream of success in the Far West. As one might expect from reading Garland's travel essays and earlier American literature, it is the Indian, Ute Jim, who initiates Harold into the mountain mysteries which point the way to his life's ultimate purpose. Garland spends considerable time developing the Natty Bumppo-Chingachgook, Ishmael-Queequeg, Lone Ranger-Tonto relationship. And good Mary must share her man with the Indians and the land.

In *The Eagle's Heart* and in Garland's other Western *Bildungsromans,* quests for success, love, and home are set against the conflicting attractions of the primitive West and civilized East. The need for arbitration between warring factions of farmers, cattlemen, sheepmen, Indians, and Mexicans adds to the conflicts in the novel. In the manner of his American hero, Teddy Roosevelt, Garland advocates dedication to duty along life's many trails. He also includes in the novel propaganda for the preservation of the land, which takes the shape of rhapsodic, lyrical tributes to the spirit of place. Garland says that Henry James wrote to him expressing his appreciation of *The Eagle's Heart.* If he was impressed with nothing else, James should have been struck by the book's multitudinousness.

Three of Garland's best romances of the Far West evidence some variations in basic patterns: *Her Mountain Lover* (1901), *Hesper* (1903), and *Money Magic* (1907). Here Garland turns to the work, love, and adventure of the miner on the trail of riches in the mountains of Colorado.

Jim Matteson, the trailer and "lover" in *Her Mountain Lover,* is in England for most of the book, trying to find a buyer for the mine he and Dr. Willard Ramsdell own on the Grizzly Bear Trail near Wagon Wheel Gap, which is a place also frequented by Black Mose. Augmenting his claim that the creation of Black Mose has priority over later Western heroes, Garland boasts that Jim Matteson "antedates by thirty years most of the somewhat similar studies of Western Americans in London" (*Companions on the Trail,* p. 13).

Matteson's search for an English buyer is complicated by homesickness for the high country and by romantic involvement with Mary Brien, a refined but somewhat "degenerate" novelist —refined and degenerate are ambivalently almost synonymous

24

for Garland here. Jim's main effort soon becomes "hitting the back trail," getting back across the Atlantic in the "big canoe," and claiming the love of Bessie, the Doctor's niece. Jim renames his mine the "Bessie B," commemorating both his love and the discovery of a new vein of ore which makes him and his bride millionaires. A clear counterpart to Harold Excell, Jim comes from Black Mose's country around Wagon Wheel and prides himself on being Mose's "brother."

Just as Harold Excell, Captain George Curtis, and Ranger Ross Cavanagh can find sanity, health, and wholeness only when they are in the Far West, so Jim Matteson, too, is almost ruined by his stay in England and regains his true identity only when back home on the Grizzly Bear Trail once again. Mary Brien, Twombly, the Englishman who almost buys the Rams-dell-Matteson mine, and England itself represent for Garland the dangerously centripetal; whereas Jim, America, and the Far West represent the expansively centrifugal.

Like so many of Garland's women, Mary longs for a strong man and wants to live in the West for her sanity and health. Somewhat like Elsie Brisbane in *The Captain,* Mary Yardwell in *The Eagle's Heart,* Ann Rupert in *Hesper,* Bertha Gilman in *Money Magic,* and Lee Virginia Wetherford in *Cavanagh Forest Ranger,* Mary Brien needs to escape the death she finds implicit in civilization and so, though equivocally, longs for the primitive Far West. Even the mock trail trip Jim takes her on in England revitalizes her, and at one point she tells Jim: "You take me to big, vital, earthly things. You make me feel the fascination of a world where clothes count for nothing, and where 'society' has no meaning. . . . Oh, I'm heart-weary of the life we call civilized. We're all rotten and dying of it. Nine-tenths of us are degenerates" (*Her Mountain Lover,* p. 152). Garland seems to preach here that behind every happy Indian and woman stands a strong, Far-West type like Matteson.

25

Matteson has seen the same parts of the Southwest that Garland saw in 1895: Santa Clara, Cañon De Shay, San Ildefonso, and "ruined cities where the streets were lined with trails six inches deep in solid rock, worn by the moccasined feet of the people that lived there" (p. 63). And it is such past trails that he identifies with his love for the mountains where, he says, "You get the first whack at the water there. Nobody above ye to poison it" (p. 170). His melodramatic love affair with Bessie is intensely linked to landscape. Going up the trail to the top of Lizard Head Peak, Jim realizes and offers his love. Standing amidst sublime clouds circling over the peak and Ouray, Bessie is overwhelmed by the "prodigious dramas" of a "marvelous upper world . . . a man's world wherein women were weak as the conies . . ." (p. 372). Jim and Bessie's climactic trail trip on the Grizzly Bear works as a structural parallel to the simulated trail trip with Mary. In both instances the style is as elevated as the locale.

Hesper (1903) is one of Garland's most complex Far-West novels, based upon Colorado's Cripple Creek mining wars. However, it too is patterned on Garland's basic trail metaphor. Growing out of Garland's numerous travels between Colorado and Wisconsin, the story, somewhat like Harold Excell's in *The Eagle's Heart*, revolves around—as Garland puts it—"a poetic lad whose determination to see the Wild West would carry him into the rude life of the border and draw with him a sister who had never been west of the Hudson River and who took pride in her ignorance of midland America" (*Hesper*, pp. i-ii). This brother-sister relationship of Louis and Ann Rupert takes shape against three groups of mining war combatants: the free miners and prospectors; the operators and mine owners of Denver and Colorado Springs; and the red-neck miners and gamblers from Denver, supported by the "mounted hoboes" from the plains.

In terms of the trail, the novel is about two "children." Being from the East, they retrace a trip their father, Philip Rupert, took West. They relive his poetic feelings about the mountains and high trails of Colorado, and rediscover their Western heritage. The brother grows up in the process and recovers from consumption, while the sister shakes off her indifference to life by falling in love with the West and with a Westerner, Rob Raymond. The action proceeds mostly by way of Garland's advancing the message that "character is a reflex to environment," a message at work to one degree or another in all his Far-Western writing. With a past closely resembling Harold Excell's, Rob Raymond escapes on the trail to the high country in search of riches and a new identity. Louis Rupert identifies with Rob and clandestinely follows him, pursued in turn by his sister Ann. Conflicts are resolved upon their meeting in the shadows cast by Mogalyon Peak, the Hesperian Mountains, and the contents of Philip Rupert's diary. Ann Rupert travels East in the closing pages of the novel only to announce her allegiance to the West and her love for and intended marriage to Raymond. Typical of Garland's formula, all trails lead higher and higher—from Valley Springs to Bozle to Sky-Town and eventually to Mogalyon Peak.

Rob Raymond, a former herder, drifter, and ranch foreman, eventually becomes a wealthy mine owner. But like Harold Excell, he has a mysterious past. Raymond too must strike it rich and prove himself worthy of Ann's love and commitment through marriage. He risks all in a mining partnership with Rocky Mountain Kelly. Like the typical Garland hero, Raymond is a clean liver, "rough but not contaminating." Raymond's changes to higher and higher station parallel Ann's return to mental health and Louis's return to physical health. Like Harold Excell, Raymond has fled a restless youth in the Midwest, at odds with his family and especially with his father, who expected a glorious military career for his son. One reason Raymond trailed West was to escape court martial for striking his West Point disciplinarian "in passion."

Villainous Jack Munro shares Raymond's secret past, which the free miner must acknowledge to Ann before he can begin his new life with her. As Munro and Raymond occupy opposing battle lines during the mining war, Raymond reveals to Barnett that Munro's real name is Jackson Hollenbeck, a classmate at West Point, expelled with Raymond for hazing and insubordination. Raymond thus sees in Louis Rupert and Munro doubles of his potentially good and bad selves. Louis and Ann, in turn, are presented with good-evil choices represented by Raymond and Munro. Although Raymond's trail upward to success and true identity stands out, Louis's and Ann's trails are even more obvious.

As a variation of Elsie Brisbane, and other of Garland's artist figures, Louis wants to illustrate animal books and, in particular, his father's journal of his trip West. It is Philip Rupert's trip which is most central to *Hesper's* structure and rendering of the West. Like Harold Excell, Jim Matteson, and others, Louis says, "I long to see what lies over that big range! That must be father's 'Hesperian Wall'. . . . It makes me want to fly like an eagle" (p. 155).

Though more her mother's child, Ann is also seeking something of "her beautiful, poetic father." Until she finds it, she asks about Louis's fascination with Western types, "What is the good of all these cheap little men and women?" (p. 23). Like Elsie Brisbane, Ann initially feels only disdain for the West. Through her love of Raymond and the spirit of place she must recapture her father's name for her, "Hesper—star of the West." She must become a part of the land her father found so beautiful. Raymond knows the meaning of Hesper in Philip Rupert's sense and becomes Ann's lover: "I can understand how he felt, for, in those days the Crestones were fabled mountains. All this country seemed a great way off—almost as remote as the place where the evening-star goes down . . ." (p. 103).

During Raymond's convalescence on Barnett's ranch, after

being shot by an interloper, he and Louis read Philip's travel journal, retracing every step, "mapping the points described as best they could," reading about the Utes and their land. It is the way Philip Rupert's journal expresses his regard for the West that brings Raymond into the sphere of Louis and Ann and makes him resolve to make something of himself. He decides to hit the high trail as the means to fulfill his resolution. Under the sublime shadow of Mogalyon, Raymond strikes it rich and gains Ann's love. Her father's journal had pointed to this peak as the restorer of health and proportion, and under the romantic spell of Mogalyon, Ann and Louis both discover the saving legacy of their father and the West.

Money Magic (1907) found considerable favor with William Dean Howells, who felt it "the most masterly of the author's books," showing through its study of the power, meaning, and limitations of wealth "that it is our conditioning which determines our characters, even though it does not always determine our actions" (W. D. Howells, "Mr. Garland's Books," *North American Review,* October 1912, pp. 527-28). Certainly this book tries hard to confirm, once again in Garland's series of romances, that a virtuous Western girl cannot be corrupted by the false snobbery and urban villainy of Eastern plutocratic matrons and lecherous artists or, for that matter, by the wealth of an older husband whose money magically exposes her to both the assets and the liabilities of refinement and culture.

More specifically, Garland wants us to know that both the West and her hard-working mother have much to do with making Bertha Gilman the kind of person she is, even after she marries Mart Haney and enters the magical world of money. She shares with Virginia Wetherford of *Cavanagh* a native Western birth. Unlike Garland's heroines of Eastern birth, Bertha discovers herself and her true heritage by travelling to the East, to her husband's home, not to the West. Haney, however, is like Garland's other heroes in being a transplanted Easterner.

Like *The Eagle's Heart, Money Magic* is another maturation story, once again structured around the idea of the trail. After she marries money out of her sense of duty, Bertha's quest is then to find love and happiness. Her husband, Captain Haney, is a familiar manifestation of Garland's Western heroes. He has years of experience as a vagabond trailer, a one-time marshal, a a gambler, and a saloon owner. But Haney is also a fair man who is torn between good and evil.

Reduced to being a semi-invalid who can only recount past glories on the trail, Haney moves for his health to the lower altitude of Colorado Springs. Settled there in a palatial house, Bertha begins her entrance into society. First she seeks recognition from the upper crust in Colorado Springs itself, then in Chicago and New York when Haney decides he must "back trail" and rediscover the family whom he fled as a youth seeking Western adventure. The trip East confirms for Bertha her love for Haney's attorney, Ben Fordyce, though she will not betray her duty to Haney. Haney senses Bertha's love for Ben, and, still heroic in his selfless love for Bertha, he commits suicide, thereby uniting Bertha and Ben.

Haney's character upstages Bertha to the point of making *Money Magic* his book. His solitary death, high in the Colorado Rockies, is the kind of Western apotheosis traditionally realized by savior gunfighters. Though sheer melodrama, it is here perversely fascinating. Haney's "Last Trail," as Garland entitles the death chapter, is a sacrifice that allows regeneration and a "new trail" for Ben and Bertha. Haney's decision to die is a hard one for him, since he has willed himself to live so enthusiastically for so long. He almost wavers when he looks into his wife's "sweet face," but "facing the west he became again the man of will" (*Money Magic*, p. 348).

His plan is to go up to his mine in the mountains, at an altitude his doctors prohibit, but nevertheless the fitting spot for the death of a high trailer. He takes only a phial of strychnine prescribed as a heart stimulant. On the train up to the mine, rumors and threats of a mining war echo about him, but he is oblivious to such battles in the face of his own. Confident that Bertha's wealth lies secure deep in the earth and remembering her as both wife and child, he whispers, " 'Tis a lonely trail I'm takin' for your sake, darlin', . . . but 'tis all for the best" (p. 351). As he reaches the crest, the sublimity of the Rockies transports him: "This was the place to die—up here where the affairs of men sank into insignificance like the sound of the mills and the rumble of trains. Here the centuries circled like swallows and the personal was lost in the ocean of silence" (p. 351).

Once off the train, he struggles up a looping trail leading to an abandoned prospector's hole. There, realizing "that he was surely hidden from all the world, he turned, poised for an instant on a mound where the trail doubled sharply, gave one long, slow glance around, then hurled himself down the rocky slope" (p. 354). His body struggles to live on for a time; then he dies the death of "the desert lion."

Undoubtedly Garland's most melodramatic utilization of the trail metaphor, Haney's death scene nevertheless incorporates some of Garland's most effective descriptive passages of the sublime magnitude of the Far-Western high country and man's consequence relative to the landscape. Most significantly, like the assimilation of Black Mose's legend into domestic respectability as Harold Excell, Haney's death represents the inevitable passing of the old West and its archetypal "free-spirited," eagle-like hero. Portrayed by Garland as fallen souls overweighed by the guilt of old ways, they are nevertheless lamented by Garland as somehow glorious, and, paradoxically, as immortal as is the spirit of place, the spirit of the Far West. Insofar as this is so, Garland's "eagles" and "lions" take on the transforming powers of the phoenix to rise again in later, more fully realized characters like Shane.

In addition to those novels which developed the prototypical hero of the American West, Garland's Far-West phase also included numerous fictional treatments of the Indian. According to James K. Folsom, "In many ways Hamlin Garland's Indian studies are a transition between traditional and modern literary treatments of the Indian" (*The American Western Novel,* p. 149). Folsom adds, "Ultimately Garland's point is that the Indian can and should be allowed to have the best of both white and red worlds" (p. 154). In attempting to "follow the red man's uneasy steps on the white man's trail," Garland treats the Indian as an individual.

"The Red Man's Present Needs" is the most explicit example of Garland's Indian views (*The North American Review,* 174 [April 1902], 476-88). The ideas he set forth in the essay are the same ideas, really, as those that pervade *The Captain of the Gray Horse Troop* and *The Book of the American Indian.* The essay is significant, too, in that as pure argument it shows Garland's reformist attitudes toward white-red relationships. The essay also provides an argumentative-persuasive norm to which the propaganda in his fiction may be compared; and it reveals Garland's stylistic and rhetorical talents as an essayist.

Written as a "policy" argument, "The Red Man's Present Needs" is a call for action involving proposed alternatives to present government practice. Establishing his credibility by identifying himself as a Western traveller and first-hand inspector of between twelve and fifteen Indian reservations, he disavows his personal political biases and claims force for his ideas through their objectivity. Although admittedly critical of the government, he maintains his intention to help rather than attack the Indian Department.

Politically, Garland divides all tribes north and south into two groups, radical and conservative, those who are willing to change and "walk in the white man's way," and those who hold on to the traditions of their race. The "conservatives" Garland regards as patriots, and he finds much to admire in their unbroken spirit. As his position in his travel writings and his Indian fiction confirms, he counts such justifiable and unconquerable pride a virtue and reminds the Department that "Hatred of tyranny is a distinctly American attribute." Garland pleads that an effort be made to conserve and turn, not break, such pride by allowing the Indian to retain his self respect. Greed, religious bigotry, and race hatred have too long confused this point, he insists. Garland is ambivalently saying that the Indian must be allowed somehow to walk the white man's trail as an Indian.

He builds the first major segment of his essay to a crescendo of emotional appeal by saying that the present treatment of the Indian is a policy based on land lust. Antagonistic to every innate desire of the Indian as it is, it is therefore doomed to failure. Such an Indian policy represents a "sombre phase of civilized life," a phase reflected in the belief that "a Stone Age man can be developed into a citizen of the United States in a single generation" (p. 479). The Sioux, he warns, should not be molded in the image of the solitary Western rancher; he is gregarious, sharing food and dwelling, in everything opposite to the assumptions behind the Dawes land theories. Such theories, Garland laments, view the Indian merely as an erring bad boy rather than a man "peculiar to his environment."

Conceding the basic assumption that the Indian must eventually walk the white man's road, Garland offers several alternatives to the present policy, alternatives that he dramatizes in his Indian fiction. First, Indian settlements should stay close to waterways on the arable and irrigable land of the reservations and not scattered by family over uplands in forced isolation. Second, each reservation should be divided into districts, with advisory farmers truly helping the Indians. Third, a field matron for each district should show the women how to cook and keep house and supplement school instruction. Fourth, qualified teacher-artists should help rescue perishing art forms, an effort essential to maintain tribal self-respect and to fulfil potential for industrial development. Fifth, children should not have to attend Eastern schools. In fact, even local sectarian schools should be closed in favor of establishing boarding and industrial schools which do not attempt to sever children from their parents. Whites and Indians should attend school together, thereby arming the red child for his "battle of life" rather than alienating him from his people. Sixth, the Indian has a right to his own kind of entertainment and recreation without interference from field missionaries who should have larger aims than making converts. Seventh, as a citizen, the Indian should be free to come and go as he pleases, subject to the same laws as white citizens; and intermarriage with other tribes, though not with whites, should be encouraged.

In general, reservation boundaries should be kept to protect the Indian from "predatory cattlemen," and abolished where ranchers become farmers with no designs on Indian land. As for exemplary models, the cowboy, though picturesque, is not a good model for the Indian to imitate, says Garland, and as a reformer and a novelist his ambivalence toward the cowboy is apparent: "The cow-boy, the 'scout,' the lawless trapper, the 'lonesome men' are passing away. As a novelist, I am sorry to see them go; as a well-wisher of the red men, and as a believer in decent speech, sobriety and kindly living, I am glad of the cowboy's diminishing hoof-beats" (p. 487).

Although capable of being read many ways, *The Captain of the Gray-Horse Troop* exemplifies the views Garland expressed more explicitly in "The Red Man's Present Needs" and is best seen as a fictionalized tract upon the Indian problem. Based on material Garland gathered in his travels West, the novel is constructed around an Indian agent's benevolent and fatherly attempts to lead his reservation wards down the white man's trail.

Captain George Curtis is Garland's spokesman in his effort to bring the "good life" to the Tetong Reservation and to himself.

A thirty-four-year-old U.S. Cavalry Captain at the time of the story, Curtis is a veteran of ten years of army duty. As an inexperienced second lieutenant, he had served in one major campaign in the Indian Wars of the 1880's. Then and at the time of the story his credo is "duty." He is present at a time of transition between the old West and the new, a point very prominent in Garland's Western fiction, and his career reflects this transition. Captain Curtis has one foot in the past as an Army officer and one in the future as an Indian agent, and he is living in the last days of the old West. The era of the President's enlightened reform of Indian policy is underway, and those policies potentially can bring "civilization" to the Tetongs. Curtis is tapped to take the Indian down the Great White Chief's trail, and he responds to duty's call with a vengeance.

As agent, Curtis must help the Indians against their foes. As a man, he must win the fiery spirit of Elsie Brisbane, an Eastern artist, to sympathize with and eventually love the Indian, the West, and himself. In terms of the novel's element of melodrama, the virtuous hero must rescue Elsie Brisbane from the evil and villainous clutches of her father, Senator Andrew Brisbane, and his racist lobby.

Curtis's and Elsie Brisbane's opposing views on the Indian "problem" are most clearly set forth in chapters nine through eleven, which deal with Curtis's trip to Washington in order to further the Tetong cause. His journey turns out to be a "trail" along which we explore political, social, and aesthetic choices arising during one of Garland's structurally important trips between East and West. Curtis travels to Washington to appear before the Committee on Indian Affairs in order to testify about the issue of removal; but the real airing of issues, the same ones aired in "The Red Man's Present Needs," takes place in the Brisbane home rather than in the Committee room. Elsie and her father see the Indian much differently than does Curtis. Elsie believes in "Light and Might," while Curtis says, "Light and Right are co-workers. Might fears both Light and Right."

His profession, he feels, guards the rights of both whites and Indians through the new policies of the government. In this light, his advice to Elsie is to face the Indian issue as an artist and a humanitarian. He criticizes one of her portraits which represents an Indian, Crawling Elk, as a beggar, not a man. Curtis's views are important, for they seem also to be Garland's ideal for rendering the Indian in art. As he looks at Elsie's picture of Crawling Elk, he says,

> This old 'beggar' . . . never lights that pipe you have put in his hands without blowing a whiff to the great spirits seated at the cardinal points of the compass. He makes offerings for the health of his children—he hears voices in the noonday haze. He sits on the hill-top at dawn to commune with the spirits over his head. As a beggar he is picturesque; as a man, he is bewildered by the changes in his world, and sad with the shadow of his children's future. All these things and many more, you must learn before you can represent the soul of the redman. You can't afford to be unjust. (*The Captain,* p. 101)

Fundamentally, Curtis-Garland preaches that art should have a moral base, whereas Elsie feels that "Art is content to add beauty to the world; it does not trouble itself to do good. It is *un*-moral" (p. 122). Curtis does succeed during the course of the novel in converting Elsie to his views about the Indian and art. However, ultimately their resolution of the issue is ambivalent, for when Elsie begins in Chapter 28 to mix a sense of duty and moral purpose with her art, Curtis comes to see the argument of art for beauty's sake. He says that in art there should be "No question of money or religion or politics," and he confesses that Elsie has instructed him in this truth.

Elsie, though, is still transformed by what Curtis taught her;

and as she recognizes her growing love for Curtis, she simultaneously realizes that she loves the West and that she has a duty to the Indian who lives there. By the time of her second trip to the Far West, her feelings toward it have modulated from wonderment to familiarity to sympathy to affection to devotion. Her conversion takes hold to the degree that she devotes herself to Curtis and his cause with the zeal of both lover and crusader: "Could there be any greater happiness than to stand by his side, helping to render a dying, captive race happier-healthier? Could her great wealth be put to better use than this of teaching two hundred thousand red people how to meet and adjust themselves to the white man's way of life?" (p. 338).

Curtis's plan to help the Tetongs is to make them herders, not farmers. By restoring their rations and attempting to implement a new policy, Curtis offers a message parallel to the hopes Garland expressed in his travel writings and "The Red Man's Present Needs": "I am your friend. . . . I come to do you good, to lead you in the new road. It is a strange road to me also, for I too am a soldier and a hunter; but together we will learn to make the earth produce meat for our eating. Put your hand in mine" (*The Captain,* p. 50).

Trouble comes when a sheepherder, Ed Cole, is found shot. Then Sheriff Winters of Piñon City attempts to wrest from Curtis his Indian ward, Cut Finger. The older chiefs like Grayman and Crawling Elk are passively reconciled to Curtis's way, and they convince the tribal council to find and give over to authorities Cole's reckless "mad fool" killer, Cut Finger. His rebellion is seen as the result of a bad head and is not condoned by any of the "responsible" Tetongs, who know such deeds are futile, part of the old West.

Yet Garland allows Cut Finger to rather majestically proclaim himself the killer and ride into the hills "to fight and die like a man." His manly resolve is, of course, no match for Curtis; and thus Garland's treatment of Cut Finger, though sympathetic, rings false. Curtis's attempt to save the Indian from a lynching mob becomes just another contrivance that allows Elsie to warn Curtis of a trap, and it provides Curtis with a showcase for his heroic deeds and military wiles as he attempts to deliver Cut Finger to the presumed safety of jail and the white man's laws. Even Cut Finger's eventual death by shooting and dragging is but another opportunity to confirm Garland's disdain for cowboys.

Victorious in love, if not completely so in war, Curtis and Elsie are soon off to Paris for a six-month honeymoon before they settle among the Tetongs to carry out Curtis's six-year plan. Before they depart, however, they preside over an intriguingly fatuous ceremony. Costumed as Indians, they witness a parade of hoe-carrying Tetongs, symbolically following Curtis's and the government's trail.

Both as a treatment of the Indian problem and as fiction, *The Book of the American Indian* surpasses *The Captain of the Gray-Horse Troop.* A collection of fourteen short stories and one novella, *The Book of the American Indian* might be considered a companion volume to Garland's other short story volumes like *Main Travelled Roads* and *They of the High Trails,* each involving a region and specific group of people. Published individually between 1899 and 1905, the stories and novella were not collected as *The Book of the American Indian* until 1923. Following the book's publication, Garland was generally credited for an innovative, first-hand, compassionate treatment of the Indian. In it he presents in fiction many of the policies and views that he had expressed earlier in "The Red Man's Present Needs" and *The Captain.* Most readers agree that these stories are examples of the best fiction in Garland's Far-Western phase.

Garland's short novel, "The Silent Eaters," compels more analysis here than the short stories which precede it. The stories are important, however, because they present a sweeping view of

Indians as individuals facing a variety of problems in finding the way along the white man's trail. The titles: "Wahiah—A Spartan Mother," "The New Medicine House," "Rising Wolf—Ghost Dancer," "Lone Wolf's Old Guard," "The Blood Lust," "The Remorse of Waumdisapa," "Drifting Crane," and "The Story of Howling Wolf" reflect this view. Each "portrait" bears out Captain George Curtis's advice to Elsie Brisbane about the basis of rendering Crawling Elk and the Indian in art: "as a man, he is bewildered by the changes in his world, and sad with the shadow of his children's future." Garland's problem in these stories is fundamentally the same as in his portrayal of Cut Finger in *The Captain*: how to allow the Indian his dignity and heritage and still assume the necessity that he must follow the white man's trail. Further, he has to find how, as a white author, to project an authentic Indian voice.

In "The Silent Eaters," Garland tries more directly to solve the problem of Indian authenticity by shifting to a first person, Indian-as-narrator point of view. Garland's typical ambivalence nevertheless accommodates the white man's point of view in that Iapi, Garland's narrative mask, is a product of the white man's schooling who has long since accepted the white way. Thus when Iapi identifies and addresses his white audience, the distance between Garland and his narrator is minimal: "There is good in all religions and all races and I am trying to write of the wrongs of my people from that point of view" (*The Book of the American Indian,* p. 222).

Ostensibly, Garland, through Iapi, is offering a biography of Sitting Bull as witnessed by one of his own people. Actually, Garland gives us an autobiography of Iapi, a red man turned white, and a spokesman for the message Garland advocates in "The Red Man's Present Needs," *The Captain,* and *The Book of the American Indian*: assimilation means survival. Iapi has his struggles and choices as a man caught between two worlds. However, the reader sees them in retrospect. The ultimate choice is already decided when Iapi recounts, for an audience he addresses as "you white men," his individual choices against the larger historical canvas of Sitting Bull's confrontation with the great white way.

Iapi's sympathies for Sitting Bull are dramatized as those held by a youth for an elder who is portrayed as a good, self-effacing man, a peacemaker, and a noble chief. To achieve this effect, Garland places Iapi in the role of a son of the leader of the Silent Eaters, a special group of advisers and guards who eat in silent council for the good of Sitting Bull and the people. Iapi, then, clearly yearns for the lost glories of his race and for his own lost youth.

Iapi's own story becomes prominent about midway in his telling of Sitting Bull's story, about the time Sitting Bull escapes with his people into Canada where Iapi, as a youngster, learns from Father Julian the white man's "wonderful sign language." Thus, by the time of Sitting Bull's captivity at Fort Randall, Iapi, with the proud blessing of his father, becomes Sitting Bull's translator and interpreter. Iapi's father counsels him to take the white trail, since the choice of the red man's trail West has ended. And in this connection, one of Garland's soldier heroes enters, Lieutenant Davies, a person like Curtis in *The Captain*. Davies befriends Iapi, tutors him in his reading, and provides Garland a voice through which to say, "Knowledge is power. . . . Study, acquire words, the white man's wisdom, then you will be able to defend the rights of your people" (p. 203).

Iapi's story includes the love of two women: Anita, fair and alluring, representative of the luxuries and mysteries of the white trail; and Oma, who speaks of the lodge fire and the sky and follows the trail of the wind. Although Anita loves Iapi and has promised to help him some day to teach the Sioux to follow the white trail, Garland mentions both her and Oma merely to dramatize the difficulty of Iapi's Indian-white choices.

Garland's own ambivalence about the Indian problem, and the choice between the primitive and the civilized way that it requires, is reflected most strongly in the way Iapi's autobiography takes over Sitting Bull's biography.

In his last days with Sitting Bull, Iapi is ashamed and alienated from his people; and yet his father and even Sitting Bull are proud of him, for he is needed during the next surge of land-hungry whites in order to listen to and interpret the commands of General Logan. And during the rapid demise of Sitting Bull, as a result of his support of the Ghost Dance, Iapi finds himself caught in the middle of a power play. The Indian agent in charge at Standing Rock plays up the rivalry for tribal leadership between The Grass, Mad Bear, and the Gall—all hoping for Sitting Bull's fall. Sitting Bull expects Iapi's allegiance in fighting the government's designs on their lands, while the agent expects Iapi to be a progressive leader of the new order. Iapi finds himself saying, "It was not easy to serve two masters, and I was forced to be in a sense double-tongued, which I did not like." Iapi is thus held suspect by both races, "deprived and rejected of both white man and red man." In effect, Iapi's "history" is an attempt to redeem the good name of Sitting Bull and to offer expiation for his own guilt and divided loyalties.

Ultimately, Garland's Indian and not his cowboy Far West earns him whatever "place in the sunset" of Western American literature he occupies. Yet certainly, with Wister, Garland "was early in the field," and his claim for priority in rendering the prototypic good-bad Western hero may be granted without viewing Black Mose as being of the same magnitude as the eponym known as the Virginian.

Garland's novels provide many examples of what Leslie Fiedler calls fused myths of the West: e.g., "love in the woods," "white woman with tomahawk," "good companions in the wilderness," and "the runaway male" (*The Return of the Vanishing American*). Some of Garland's works contain the hunter and captivity mythology of the frontier, a subject analyzed by Richard Slotkin in *Regeneration Through Violence*. The Western formulas that John G. Cawelti discusses in *Six Gun Mystique* also abound in Garland's fictional treatments of cowboys and Indians.

Assuredly one cannot completely separate Indian from cowboy concerns in the Far West. As an author from a white, Midwestern farm family who believed that their group destiny was to clear the wilderness and subdue the savage, Garland inherently must, in his literary and actual journeys to the Far West, make his own errand in the wilderness, and reconcile himself with both the Indian and the cowboy. But, taken all in all, the salient presence of Native Americans in Garland's Far West gives him more than a limited degree of stature as a Western author. His contribution to the literary heritage of the West is significant if we grant Fiedler's contention "that tales set in the West seem to us not quite Westerns, unfulfilled occasions for myth rather than myth itself, when no Indian . . . appears in them" (*The Return of the Vanishing American*, p. 24). Not only Garland's concern for and empathy with the Native American, but also the time of the expression of that concern is why Garland matters most in the Western American literary tradition.

Garland's Indian studies form part of his exploration in his travel writings, essays, and novels of the meaning of life in the Far West. The relationships between his actual and imaginative journeys can be seen, as I have shown, in the centrality of travel, the spirit of place, and the trail metaphor with its associated characters, themes, imagery, and tone in his life and work.

Garland's Far-West writings represent a continuation of his own "Abner Joyce" myth as satirically but accurately portrayed by Henry Blake Fuller. These writings need not be viewed as aberrant romances, the apostasy of a "veritist," for they offer insight into the shifting boundaries of the West as locale and as idea at the turn of the century. In the passage through what became his Far West, Garland rediscovered and redefined the Midwest in a way which would lead him to his masterwork, *A Son of the Middle Border,* a work which would decisively earn for him the right to be regarded as an authentic "literary pioneer of the West."

Selected Bibliography

NOTE: Garland's published works run to more than 300 titles; and at least 40 of these titles are book length. This bibliography is limited primarily to selected Western writings; however, other selected works are also mentioned. For a more complete listing of Garland's works see the bibliographies listed here.

Essays by Garland

"Among the Moki Indians." *Harper's Weekly,* 40 (August 15, 1896), 801-07.

"Automobiling in the West." *Harper's Weekly,* 46 (September 6, 1902), 1254-55.

"A Day at Isleta." *Southwestern Historical Quarterly,* 78 (July 1974), 45-68.

"General Custer's Last Fight as Seen by Two Moon." *McClure's Magazine* 11 (September 1898), 443-48.

"Hitting the Trail." *McClure's Magazine,* 12 (February 1899), 298-304.

"Ho, for the Klondike!" *McClure's Magazine,* 10 (March 1898), 443-54.

"Into the Happy Hunting-Grounds of the Utes." *Harper's Weekly,* 40 (April 1896), 350-51.

"The Red Man's Present Needs." *The North American Review,* 174 (April 1902), 476-88. Reprinted in *The North American Review,* 258 (Winter 1973), 90-95.

"Sanity in Fiction." *The North American Review,* 176 (March 1903), 336-48.

"The West in Literature." *Arena,* 6 (November 1892), 669-76.

"Western Landscapes." *Atlantic Monthly,* 72 (December 1893), 805-09.

Short Fiction by Garland

"A Night Raid at Eagle River." *Century Magazine,* 76 (September 1908), 725-34.

45

The Book of the American Indian. New York: Harper & Brothers, 1923.
"Delmar of Pima." *McClure's Magazine,* 18 (February 1902), 340-48.
"Sitting Bull's Defiance." *McClure's Magazine,* 20 (November 1902), 35-40.
They of the High Trails. New York: Harper & Brothers, 1916.

Novels by Garland

The Captain of the Gray-Horse Troop. New York: Harper & Brothers,
 1902. Reprinted by Greg Press, 1970.
Cavanagh Forest Ranger. New York: Harper & Brothers, 1910.
The Eagle's Heart. New York: D. Appleton & Co., 1900.
The Forester's Daughter. New York: Harper & Brothers, 1914.
Her Mountain Lover. New York: Grosset & Dunlap, 1901.
Hesper. New York: Harper & Brothers, 1903.
The Light of the Star. New York: Harper & Brothers, 1904.
The Long Trail. New York: Harper & Brothers, 1907.
Money Magic. New York: Harper & Brothers, 1907.
The Moccasin Ranch. New York: Harper & Brothers, 1909. Republished
 by Scholarly Press, 1974.
The Spirit of Sweetwater. New York: Doubleday & McClure's, 1898.
Victor Olnee's Discipline. New York: Harper & Brothers, 1911.

Poetry by Garland

Iowa, O Iowa. Iowa City: Clio Press, 1935.
"The Trail to the Golden North." *McClure's Magazine,* 12 (April 1899),
 505-07; and 13 (May 1899), 65-67.
"The Ute Lover." *The Century Magazine,* 58 (June 1899), 218-20.

Autobiographies by Garland

Afternoon Neighbors. New York: Macmillan, 1934.
Back-Trailers from the Middle Border. New York: Macmillan, 1928.
Boy Life on the Prairie. New York: Macmillan, 1899.
Companions on the Trail. New York: Macmillan, 1931.
A Daughter of the Middle Border. New York: Macmillan, 1921.
Hamlin Garland's Diaries, ed. Donald Pizer. San Marino: The Huntington
 Library, 1968.
My Friendly Contemporaries. New York: Macmillan, 1932.
Roadside Meetings. New York: Macmillan, 1930.
A Son of the Middle Border. New York: Macmillan, 1917.

Miscellaneous by Garland

Prairie Song and Western Story: Selections. Boston: Allyn & Bacon, 1928. Reprinted by Books for Libraries Press, 1971.

Westward March of American Settlement. Chicago: American Library Association, 1927.

Critical Studies and Secondary Sources

Ahnebrink, Lars. *The Beginnings of Naturalism in American Fiction, 1891-1903.* New York: Russell & Russell, 1961.

Duffey, Bernard I. "Hamlin Garland's 'Decline' from Realism." *American Literature,* 25 (March 1953), 69-74.

Fiedler, Leslie A. *The Return of the Vanishing American.* New York: Stein & Day, 1968.

Folsom, James K. *The American Western Novel.* New Haven: College & University Press, 1966.

French, Warren. "What Shall We Do About Hamlin Garland?" *American Literary Realism,* 4 (Fall 1970), 283-89.

Fuller, Henry Blake. "The Downfall of Abner Joyce." *Under the Skylights.* New York: D. Appleton, 1901. Reprinted by Garrett Press, 1969.

Hamlin Garland, A Son of the Middle Border. New York: Macmillan, n.d. (Promotion Pamphlet)

Holloway, Jean. *Hamlin Garland: A Biography.* Austin: University of Texas Press, 1960.

Howells, William Dean. "Mr. Garland's Books." *North American Review,* 19 (October 1912), 523-28.

Keiser, Albert. *The Indian in American Literature.* New York: Oxford University Press, 1933.

Mane, Robert. *Hamlin Garland, L'homme et l'oeuvre (1860-1940).* Paris: Didier, 1968.

Martin, Jay. *Harvests of Change: American Literature, 1865-1914.* Englewood Cliffs: Prentice-Hall, 1967.

Marovitz, Sanford. " 'Romance or Realism?' Western Periodical Literature: 1893-1902." *Western American Literature,* 10 (May 1975), 46-58.

McCann, William. "Hamlin Garland." *Encyclopedia of American Biography.* New York: Harper & Row, 1974. Pp. 404-05.

Meyer, Roy W. "Hamlin Garland and the American Indian." *Western American Literature,* 2 (Summer 1967), 109-25.

Miller, Charles T. "Hamlin Garland's Retreat from Realism." *Western American Literature,* 1 (Summer 1966), 119-29.

Neumann, Edwin J. "Hamlin Garland and the Mountain West." Unpublished Doctoral Dissertation, Northwestern University, 1957.

Pizer, Donald. "Hamlin Garland (1860-1940)." *American Literary Realism,* 1 (Fall 1967), 45-51.

Reamer, Owen J. "Garland and the Indians." *New Mexico Quarterly,* 34 (Autumn 1964), 257-80.

Underhill, Lonnie E. and Littlefield, Daniel F., eds. "Hamlin Garland at Isleta Pueblo." *Southwestern Historical Quarterly,* 78 (July 1974), 45-68.

Walcutt, Charles. *American Literary Naturalism, A Divided Stream.* Minneapolis: University of Minnesota Press, 1956.

Ziff, Larzer. *The American 1890's: Life and Times of a Lost Generation.* New York: The Viking Press, 1966.

Bibliographies

Arvidson, Lloyd A. *Hamlin Garland: Centennial Tributes and A Checklist of the Hamlin Garland Papers in the University of Southern California Library.* Los Angeles: University of Southern California Library Bulletin No. 9, 1962.

Bryer, Jackson R. and Harding, Eugene. *Hamlin Garland and the Critics, An Annotated Bibliography.* Troy: Whitson Publishing Co., 1973. Also see *American Literary Realism,* 3 (Fall 1970), 290-387.

Etulain, R. W. *Western American Literature: A Bibliography of Interpretive Books and Articles.* Vermillion: Dakota Press, 1972. Pp. 67-68.

Pizer, Donald. *Hamlin Garland's Early Work and Career.* Berkeley: University of California Press, 1960.